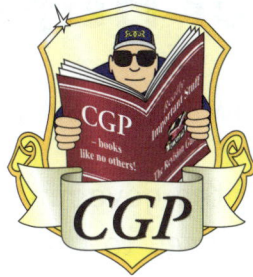

Phonics Activity Book

for ages 3-4

This CGP book is bursting with bright and colourful Phonics activities for pre-school children.

It's a brilliant way to introduce the essential skills — and it's stacks of fun too!

Hints for Helpers

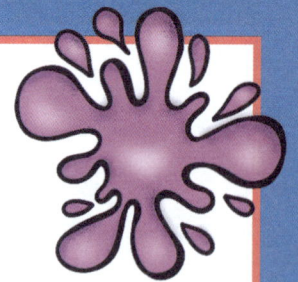

Here are a few useful things to know when using this book:

- This book covers **Phase Two** of the government's **'Letters and Sounds'** programme, which is often introduced to children at **Nursery** or **Pre-school**, and is also taught in **Reception**.

- The book helps children to practise some of the most common **sounds** in the English language and recognise the **letters** that are usually used to write these sounds.

- This book is designed to be worked through in **order**. However, the 'Hide-and-seek' activity in the centre uses sounds from the **whole book** — you may want to save this activity until last.

- Learning to **listen carefully** is an important part of learning Phonics. Children should be encouraged to say **aloud** what they think a picture is, and to **listen** to the sounds that they make as they say the word. This is great practice, even if they're not ready to start **reading** for themselves yet.

- You could also try saying the words in this book aloud **yourself** and encouraging your child to **repeat** the sounds they hear.

- Once your child is beginning to tackle reading whole words, encourage them to **segment** each word into individual sounds, then **blend** the sounds together to read the whole word.

- For example, to read the word 'sat', they should **segment** the word into separate sounds — 's', 'a' and 't', which sound like 'ss', 'a' and 'tuh'.

- They should then **blend** these letter sounds together ('ss-a-tuh') to work out how to say the whole word.

- A sound can sometimes be written using **more than one letter**, such as the 'll' in 'doll'. These sounds are underlined.

- Generally, it is helpful to use **letter sounds** with your child, rather than **letter names**. For example, if you see the letter 'b' you should say 'buh', not 'bee'.

Contents

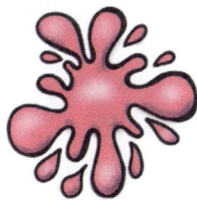

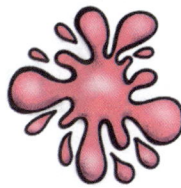

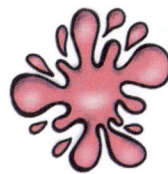

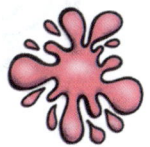

Published by CGP

Editors: Izzy Bowen, Andy Cashmore, Rachel Craig-McFeely, Emma Crighton, Adam Worster

With thanks to Sharon Gulliver and Holly Robinson for the proofreading.

With thanks to Jan Greenway for the copyright research.

ISBN: 978 1 78908 607 2

Printed by Elanders Ltd, Newcastle upon Tyne.
Cover and graphics used throughout the book © www.edu-clips.com
Cover design concept by emc design ltd.

Text, design, layout and original illustrations © Coordination Group Publications Ltd. (CGP) 2020
All rights reserved.

s, t and a

How It Works

Say aloud what the pictures are and listen to the sounds you say.

sun

tap

ant

Now listen for these sounds as you say them again — **s**, **t** and **a**.

Now Try These

Circle the picture that starts with the **s** sound.

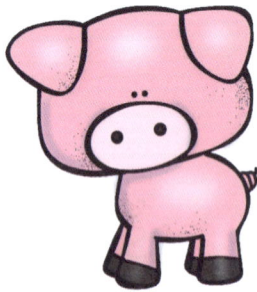

Put a tick under the fruit that starts with the **a** sound.

☐ ☐ ☐

2

Colour the animal that starts with the **s** sound.

Can you spot two things in the picture that start with the **t** sound?

Draw lines to match each picture to the sound it starts with.

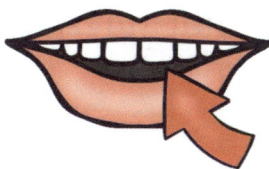

s   **a**   **t**

You did that so well it's baa-rmy! Colour the smiley face.

3

p, n and i

Remember to say aloud what the pictures are and listen to the sounds you say.

How It Works

Practise saying the **p**, **n** and **i** sounds.

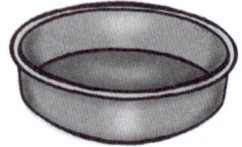

pan

nap

t**i**n

Now Try These

Colour the picture that starts with the **p** sound.

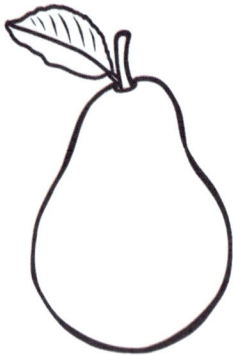

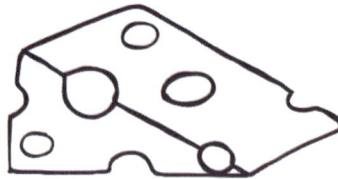

What things can you see in the picture? Say them aloud.
Can you spot **two** things that have the **i** sound?

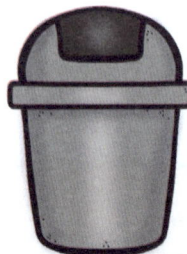

Put a tick under the picture that starts with the **n** sound.

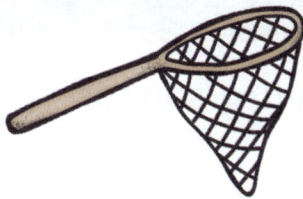

☐   ☐   ☐

Which colour of ice cream starts with the **p** sound?
Draw a line to match it to the **p**.

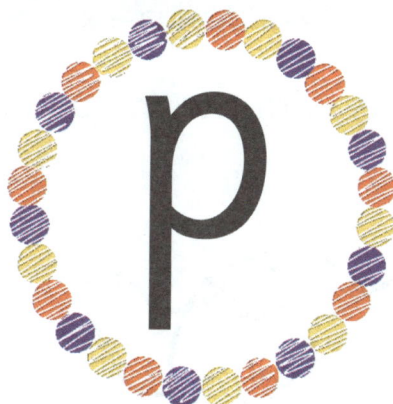

p

What is Kim using to stir her cake mixture?
Say the word. Draw a circle around the sound you can hear.

i   n

You made that look like a piece of cake! Colour the smiley face.

5

m, d and g

How It Works

Practise saying the **m**, **d** and **g** sounds.

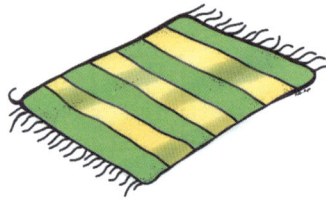

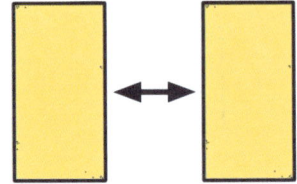

mat   **d**en   **g**ap

Now Try These

Colour the picture that starts with the **m** sound.

Can you spot two things in the room that start with the **d** sound?

Circle the picture that starts with a **g** sound.

Draw lines to match each picture to the sound it starts with.

g   m   d

What sound do all these words start with? Circle the right answer.

d   g   m

You've mastered these sounds! Colour the smiley face.

7

Word practice

How It Works

Practise blending sounds together to make words.

Break a word down into its different sounds.
Then blend the sounds together to say the whole word.

 S - a - m ➡ Sam

Now Try These

Practise saying the words below.
Draw lines to match each picture to the sound it starts with.

dip

map

pin

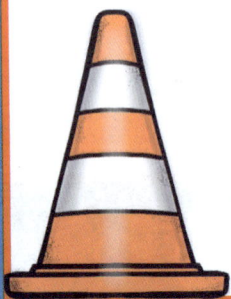

d

m

p

Say the words below. Draw lines to match
each word to the picture it describes.

dig   tip   man

Practise saying the words, then finish colouring in the picture.

sat   sip   Tim

Phew, that was hard work — well done! Colour the smiley face.

Hide-and-seek

Let's play hide-and-seek! Use the clues to find each person, then finish colouring in the picture.

You'll need sounds from the whole book to do this activity.

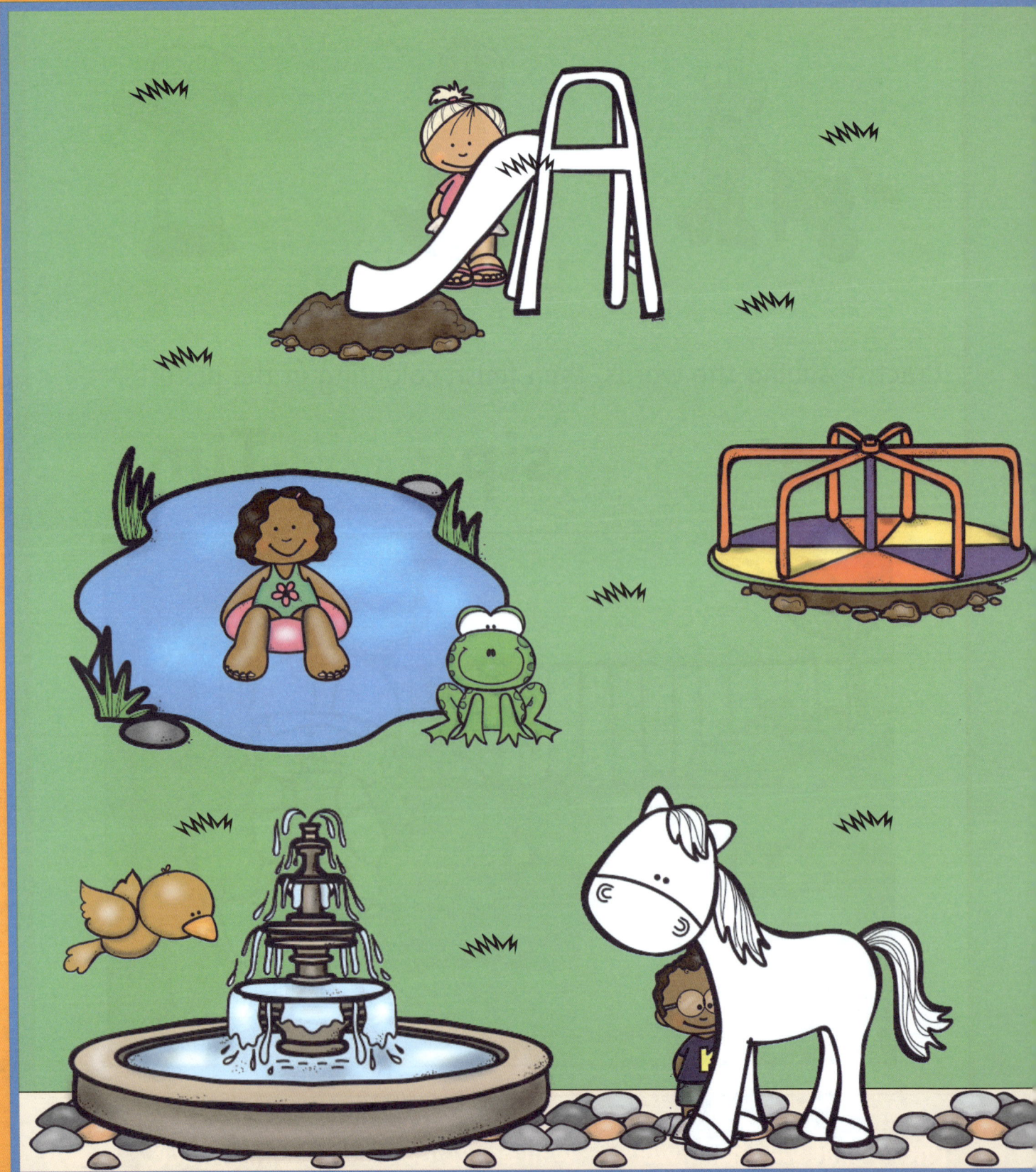

h	Stan is hiding behind an animal that starts with this sound.

s	Jo is hiding behind something that starts with this sound.

c	Mimi is hiding in a building that starts with this sound.

b	Tim is hiding in something that takes you to places. It starts with this sound.

BUS STOP

o, c and k

How It Works

Practise saying **o**, **c** and **k**.

on

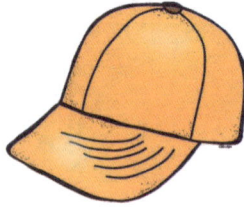

cap

kid

c and **k** make the same sound.

Now Try These

Put a tick under the picture that starts with the **k** sound.

☐

☐

☐

Circle the picture that starts with the **o** sound.

Which picture starts with the **c** sound?
Draw a line to match it to the **c**.

Colour the picture that starts with the **k** sound.

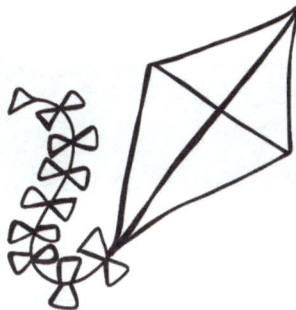

Can you spot two things in the picture that start with the **c** sound?

You've sprung through these pages! Colour the smiley face.

13

ck, e and u

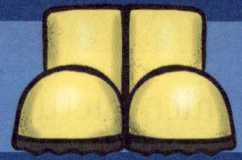

How It Works

Practise saying the **ck**, **e** and **u** sounds.

so**ck**   e**gg**   **u**p

ck makes the same sound as **c** and **k** do on their own. You'll never see **ck** at the start of a word — only the middle or the end.

Now Try These

What is this picture?
Say the word, then circle the letter or letters it ends with.

e   ck

Can you spot something in the picture that starts with an **e** sound?

14

Which picture starts with the **u** sound?
Draw a line to match it to the **u**.

Colour the picture blue if it ends with the **ck** sound.
Colour the picture green if it starts with the **e** sound.

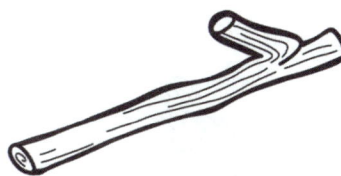

Put a tick under the picture that contains the **u** sound.

You've blown through these pages! Colour the smiley face.

15

r, h and b

Have a go at saying the **r**, **h** and **b** sounds.

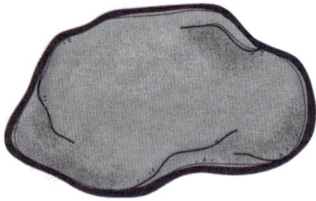

ro<u>ck</u>   **h**op   **b**un

Draw a circle around the picture that starts with the **r** sound.

Which food starts with the **h** sound?
Draw a line to match it to the **h**.

16

Ben is having a picnic.
Colour the food that starts with the **b** sound.

Put a tick under the picture that starts with the **h** sound.

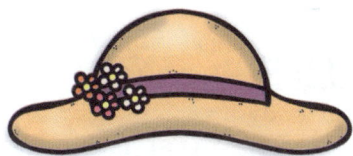

☐   ☐   ☐

Colour the picture red if it starts with the **r** sound.
Colour the picture blue if it starts with the **b** sound.

Was this page a walk in the park? Colour the smiley face.

17

f, ff, l, ll and ss

f and **ff** make the same sound.   **l** and **ll** make the same sound.

fan   pu**ff**   **l**og   do**ll**

Now practise saying **ss**.

pu**ss**

Put a tick under the picture that starts with the **l** sound.

☐   ☐   ☐

Colour the picture that starts with the **f** sound.

Say the word for each picture. What sounds can you hear at the **end** of the words? Join each picture to the correct letters.

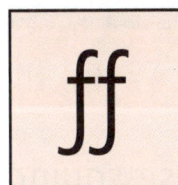

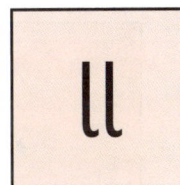

ff

ll

Say what the cat is sitting on. What sound can you hear at the end of the word? Circle the right letters.

ss   ff

Wow, your sounds are purr-fect! Colour the smiley face.

19

Word practice

How It Works

Now mix the sounds you've learnt to make words.

Say the letter sounds in the word very carefully.
Then, blend the sounds together to say the whole word.

p – e – t ➡ pet

Now Try These

Practise saying the words below.
Draw lines to match each word to the picture it describes.

mum **bed** **cup**

Can you say the words below?
Then finish colouring in the picture.

hug

bat

Pam

Say the words below.
Draw lines to match each word to the picture it describes.

kiss   nan   mud

Well done — you're brilliant! Colour the smiley face.

Word practice

Here are some more words for you to try.
Think about the sound each word starts with.

Now Try These

It's Sports Day! Say the words below, then colour in the picture that matches each word.

run

hop

sit

kick

Well done — you raced through that! Colour the smiley face.

EPFEOQ01